The Child's Story

ADAPTED FROM THE STORY BY

CHARLES DICKENS

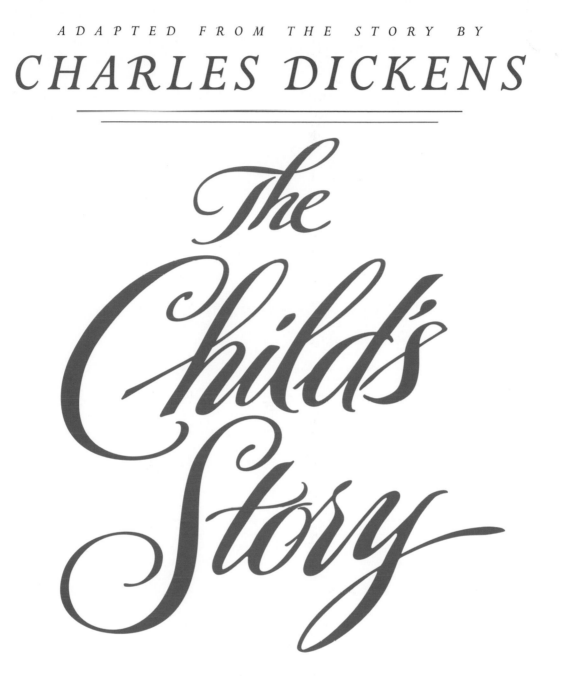

The Child's Story

PAINTINGS BY

HARVEY CHAN

SIMON & SCHUSTER BOOKS FOR YOUNG READERS

New York   London   Toronto   Sydney   Singapore

*"It is one of my rules in life not to
believe a man who may happen to tell me
that he feels no interest in children . . ."*

—CHARLES DICKENS, 1858

*To all those who allow me to share
the wisdom of their journeys*

—H.C.

SIMON & SCHUSTER
BOOKS FOR YOUNG READERS
An imprint of Simon & Schuster Children's Publishing Division
1230 Avenue of the Americas, New York, New York 10020

Text copyright © 2000 by Simon & Schuster
Illustrations copyright © 2000 by Harvey Chan
SIMON & SCHUSTER BOOKS FOR YOUNG READERS is a trademark of Simon & Schuster.
Book design by Heather Wood
The text for this book is set in Golden Cockerel. The illustrations are rendered in oil pastels.
Printed in Hong Kong
2 4 6 8 10 9 7 5 3 1

Library of Congress Cataloging-in-Publication Data
Dickens, Charles, 1812-1870.
The child's story / adapted from Charles Dickens; illustrated by Harvey Chan.
p.   cm.
Cover title: Charles Dickens's The Child's Story
Summary: An old man recalls the different stages of his life as a journey that he shares with his grandchildren.
ISBN 0-689-83482-9
[1. Grandfathers—Fiction.] I. Title: Charles Dickens's The Child's Story. II. Chan, Harvey, ill. III. Title.
PZ7.D55 Ce 2000   [E]—dc21   99-46446

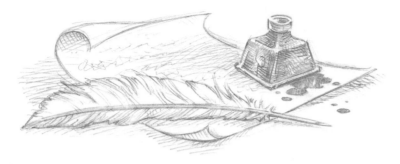

FOREWORD

Dickens's fascination with children and his talent for awakening that fascination in others can be easily demonstrated by any list of his most popular fictional creations. Oliver Twist, Little Nell, David Copperfield, Tiny Tim—these are all children vivid enough to have captured adult audiences from the minute their stories were published. Orphans usually, imperiled always, these children still keep alive their innocence and imagination, qualities that for Dickens defined childhood. So it might almost be said that every one of Dickens's stories is "a child's story," a story about one child's passage into and through an adult world that threatens to overwhelm the freshness of a child's original vision. Dickens's own childhood, marred by poverty and early solitude, was no model of happiness, but in much of his writing childhood is a charmed place where perception and judgment are magically true. The appeal of this theme made Dickens perhaps the last great novelist who succeeded in equal measure with children and their elders.

Therefore one could argue that Dickens's greatest accomplishment was to invent the idea of the child as we now have it. No longer unformed adults to be seen and not heard, or even *not* seen and not heard, Dickens's children represent the innocence and optimism that sustains each of us as the world that surrounds us becomes ever more vast and complex. It is no surprise that so much of his writing, like this volume, is expressly for children—and for adults who want to eavesdrop on the enchantment that, for Dickens, was the story of childhood.

NICHOLAS DAMES

Columbia University

nce upon a time, a good many years ago, there was a traveller, and he set out upon a journey. It was a magic journey, and was to seem very long when he began it, and very short when he got halfway through.

He travelled along a rather dark path for some little time, without meeting anything, until at last he came to a beautiful child. So he said to the child, "What do you do here?" And the child said, "I am always at play. Come and play with me!"

So, he played with that child, the whole day long, and they were very merry. The sky was so blue, the sun was so bright, the water was so sparkling, the leaves were so green, the flowers were so lovely, and they heard such singing-birds and saw so many butterflies, that everything was beautiful. This was in fine weather.

When it rained, they loved to watch the falling drops, and to smell the fresh scents.

When it blew, it was delightful to listen to the wind, and fancy what it said, as it came rushing from its home—where was that, they wondered!—whistling and howling, driving the clouds before it, bending the trees, rumbling in the chimneys, shaking the house, and making the sea roar in fury.

But, when it snowed, that was the best of all; for, they liked nothing so well as to look up at the white flakes, falling fast and thick, like down from the breasts of millions of white birds; and to see how smooth and deep the drift was and listen to the hush upon the paths and roads.

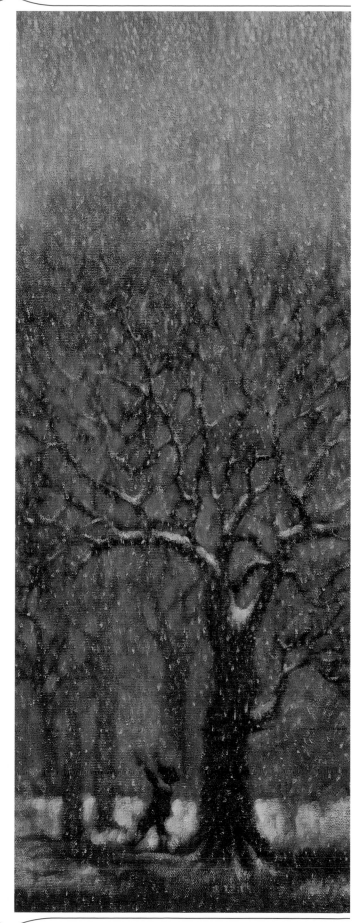

They had plenty of the finest toys in the world, and the most astonishing picture-books: all about scimitars and slippers and turbans, and dwarfs and giants and genii and fairies, and blue-beards and bean-stalks and riches and caverns and forests and Valentines and Orsons: and all new and all true.

But, one day, of a sudden, the traveller lost the child. He called to him over and over again, but got no answer. So, he went upon his road, and went on for a little while without meeting anything, until at last he came to a handsome boy. So, he said to the boy, "What do you do here?" And the boy said, "I am always learning. Come and learn with me."

So he learned with that boy about Jupiter and Juno, and the Greeks and the Romans, and I don't know what, and learned more than I could tell—or he either, for he soon forgot a great deal of it. But, they were not always learning; they had the merriest games that ever were played. They rowed upon the river in summer, and skated on the ice in winter; they were active afoot, and active on horseback, at cricket, and all games at ball; at prisoners' base, hare and hounds, follow my leader,

and more sports than I can think of; nobody could beat them. They had holidays too, and Twelfth cakes, and parties where they danced till midnight, and real Theatres where they saw palaces of real gold and silver rise out of the real earth, and saw all the wonders of the world at once. As to friends, they had such dear friends and so many of them, that I want the time to reckon them up. They were all young, like the handsome boy, and were never to be strange to one another again.

Still, one day, in the midst of all these pleasures, the traveller lost the boy as he had lost the child, and, after calling to him in vain, went on upon his journey. So he went on for a little while without seeing anything, until at last he came to a young man. So, he said to the young man, "What do you do here?"

And the young man said, "I am always in love. Come and love with me."

So, he went away with that young man, and presently they came to one of the prettiest girls that was ever seen. So, the young man fell in love directly.

Well! He was teased sometimes; and they quarrelled sometimes; and they made it up, and sat in the dark, and wrote letters every day, and never were happy asunder, and were always looking out for one another and pretending not to, and were engaged at Christmastime, and sat close to one another by the fire, and were going to be married very soon.

But, the traveller lost them one day, as he had lost the rest of his friends, and, after calling to them to come back, which they never did, went on upon his journey. So, he went on for a little while without seeing anything, until at last he came to a middle-aged gentleman. So, he said to the gentleman, "What are you doing here?" And his answer was, "I am always busy. Come and be busy with me!"

So, he began to be very busy with that gentleman, and they went on through the wood together. The whole journey was through a wood, only it had been open and green at first, like a wood in spring; and now began to be thick and dark, like a wood in summer; some of the little trees that had come out earliest, were even turning brown. The gentleman was not alone, but had a lady of about the same age with him, who was his Wife; and they had children, who were with them too. So, they all went on together through the wood, cutting down the trees, and making a path through the branches and the fallen leaves, and carrying burdens, and working hard.

Sometimes, they came to a long green avenue that opened into deeper woods. Then they would hear a very little, distant voice crying, "Father, father, I am another child! Stop for me!" And presently they would see a very little figure, growing larger as it came along, running to join them. When it came up, they all crowded round it, and kissed and welcomed it; and then they all went on together.

Sometimes, they came to several avenues at once, and then they all stood still, and one of the children said, "Father, I am going to sea," and another said, "Father, I am going to India," and another, "Father, I am going to seek my fortune where I can," and another, "Father, I am going to Heaven!" So, with many tears at parting, they went, solitary, down those avenues, each child upon its way; and the child who went to Heaven, rose into the golden air and vanished.

Whenever these partings happened, the traveller looked at the gentleman, and saw him glance up at the sky above the trees, where the day was beginning to decline, and the sunset to come on. He saw, too, that his hair was turning grey. But, they never could rest long, for they had their journey to perform, and it was necessary for them to be always busy.

At last, there had been so many partings that there were no children left, and only the traveller, the gentleman, and the lady, went upon their way in company. And now the wood was yellow; and now brown; and the leaves, even of the forest trees, began to fall.

So, they came to an avenue that was darker than the rest, and were pressing forward on their journey without looking down it when the lady stopped.

"My husband," said the lady. "I am called."

They listened, and they heard a voice a long way down the avenue, say, "Mother, mother!"

It was the voice of the first child who had said, "I am going to Heaven!" and the father said, "I pray not yet. The sunset is very near. I pray not yet!"

But, the voice cried, "Mother, mother!" without minding him, though his hair was now quite white, and tears were on his face.

Then, the mother, who was already drawn into the shade of the dark avenue and moving away with her arms still round his neck, kissed him, and said, "My dearest, I am summoned, and I go!" And she was gone. And the traveller and he were left alone together.

And they went on and on together, until they came to very near the end of the wood: so near, that they could see the sunset shining red before them through the trees.

Yet, once more, while he broke his way among the branches, the traveller lost his friend. He called and called, but there was no reply, and when he passed out of the wood, and saw the peaceful sun going down upon a wide purple prospect, he came to an old man sitting on a fallen tree. So, he said to the old man, "What do you do here?" And the old man said with a calm smile, "I am always remembering. Come and remember with me!"

So the traveller sat down by the side of that old man, face to face with the serene sunset; and all his friends came softly back and stood around him. The beautiful child, the handsome boy, the young man in love, the father, mother, and children: every one of them was there, and he had lost nothing.

So, he loved them all, and was kind and forbearing
with them all, and was always pleased to watch them all,
and they all honoured and loved him.

And I think the traveller must be yourself,
dear Grandfather,
because this is what you do to us,
and what we do to you.